WORLD BOOK
looks at
INSECTS AND SPIDERS

World Book, Inc.
a Scott Fetzer Company
Chicago   London   Sydney   Toronto

WORLD BOOK
looks at
INSECTS AND SPIDERS

World Book Looks At

Books in this series are based on information and illustrations contained in The World Book Encyclopedia.

Created and edited by Brian Williams and Brenda Williams.
Designed by Tim Mayer.

World Book, Inc.
525 W. Monroe
Chicago, Illinois 60661

For information on other World Book products, call 1-800-255-1750, extension 3771.

ISBN: 0-7166-1800-1 (hard cover)
ISBN: 0-7166-1806-0 (soft cover)
Library of Congress Catalog Card Number 96-62475

Printed in Mexico

1 2 3 4 5 6 7 8 9 10 99 98 97 96

CONTENTS

Introducing Insects and Spiders

The honey bee sucks nectar from flowers. Without insects, our world would not have so many flowering plants.

They scuttle across the floor. They hide under rocks. They buzz around the picnic basket. They're insects.

Insects live almost everywhere. You might not always see them, because they are so small. But there are lots of them around. In fact, more of these creepy-crawly creatures live in our world than any other kind of animal!

What is an insect?

An insect is a small animal with six legs. Lots of other animals we think of as creepy-crawlies or bugs are not insects. A worm is not an insect. A slug is not an insect. A wood louse is not an insect.

Is a spider an insect?

No, a spider is a different kind of animal altogether. A spider has eight legs, not six. Its body is a different shape too. Many spiders live by hunting insects. So where there are insects, you find spiders.

Insects everywhere

Insects come in all shapes and sizes. Some insects are beautiful. Some look scary. Some insects run about, some fly, and some burrow in the ground. They have many ways of finding food, making homes, and escaping from their enemies.

Insects and spiders are fascinating animals. Let's take a closer look at their world.

The tarantula is one of the biggest spiders. Some people keep tarantulas as pets!

The treehopper is an odd-looking animal. Like many insects, it feeds on plants.

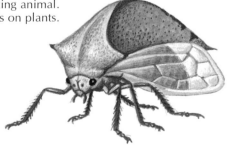

PUZZLED BY A WORD?

To learn the meaning of a difficult or new word, turn to the glossary on page 62.

More and more insects

- Scientists have named more than one million species, or kinds, of animals. Most of them are insects. In fact, only about 44,000 of these animal species are not insects!

- From 7,000 to 10,000 new kinds of insects are discovered every year!

- Thousands of other insect species live – unknown as yet – in forests, deserts, and mountains. Scientists believe that the complete list of insect species could number over 10 million!

A beautiful moth from the island of Madagascar in the Indian Ocean. Some insects are brilliantly colored.

Scale insects may look like buttons, but they are sucking insects.

The mayfly appears in summer – the best time to spot most insects. But be quick – the adult mayfly lives for only a few hours.

The rhinoceros beetle is named for the horn on its head. Luckily, this beetle is not as big as a rhinoceros. Beetles make up the most numerous group of insects.

5

An Amazing World

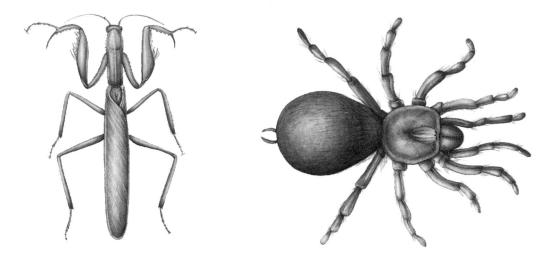

How to tell an insect from a spider

Look carefully at the pictures. On the left you see a praying mantis, and on the right you see a trap-door spider. The mantis is an insect – it has six legs. The spider has eight legs. An insect's body has three main parts: head, thorax (middle), and abdomen. A spider's body has just two parts, a head and thorax joined and an abdomen. Most insects also have a pair of antennae or feelers, and many insects have wings. Spiders have no antennae and no wings.

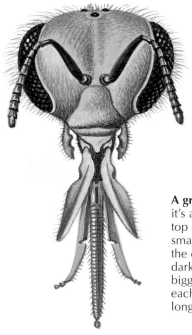

A grouchy-looking alien? No, it's a friendly worker bee. On top of its head, the bee has small simple eyes that can tell the difference between darkness and daylight. It has bigger compound eyes on each side of its head, and a long red tongue.

Good to eat

All spiders have fangs, and most kinds of spiders have poison glands. A spider's bite can kill an insect. Spiders eat grasshoppers, locusts, flies, and mosquitoes.

Insects are tough

Insects are small, but amazingly tough. Many have enormous strength for their size. They can easily lift more than their own weight. They could out sprint and out jump an Olympic athlete.

Humans have fewer than 700 muscles. A tiny caterpillar may have as many as 4,000 muscles.

Insects can live in water as cold as ice. Some insects have come back to life after being frozen solid. They just had to be thawed out.

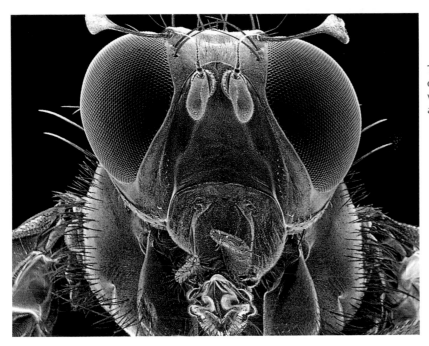

The face of a fruit fly – magnified of course. It has huge eyes, as well as hairs and spines that serve as touch organs.

An insect's body is inside out!

Insects have their skeletons on the outside of their bodies! This kind of skeleton is called an exoskeleton. It is made of material lighter yet stronger than bone.

Insects have mouths adapted either for chewing or sucking.

Insect blood is not red – it is greenish, yellowish, or colorless. Insects are cold-blooded animals.

An insect breathes air through holes along the sides of its body. These holes are called spiracles.

Seeing, smelling, flying

Most adult insects have two enormous compound eyes. These eyes are made up of lots of separate lenses. Most insects see well, but only over short distances.

Almost all insects have two antennae. They use their antennae chiefly to smell and to feel.

Insects are the only animals besides birds and bats that have wings.

The head of a male moth. The feathery "feelers" are its antennae. The male moth uses its antennae to find female partners. When the antennae catch the scent of a female, the male flies off to find her.

Arthropods All

All insects belong to the large group of animals called arthropods. The name arthropod comes from two Greek words meaning "jointed feet." Actually, an insect's legs – not its feet – are jointed. All arthropods have jointed legs. The insects make up the largest class of arthropods. Spiders are arthropods too.

Armored battlers

These battling stag beetles have long jaws and armored bodies. They live in Europe. The tough outside of an insect's body is made of several substances, including a stiff, horny material called chitin. Chitin is the armor that protects the insect's soft inner parts. When an insect grows too big for its old armor suit, it grows a new one underneath and then crawls out of the old one.

Arctic bumblebee

Can insects live in the Arctic?

More insects live in the Arctic than in the Antarctic. The Arctic has more plants (over 1,000 kinds) including grasses, mosses and flowers such as poppies. These plants provide food and shelter for flies and other insects, including bees. The Antarctic has few plants, and so is not a good home for insects. A tiny wingless midge (a kind of fly) does manage to live there though.

An insect lion

Despite its name, the ant lion could not be mistaken for a big cat – though it is a crafty hunter. The ant lion is the larva, or immature form, of an insect that grows up to look like a dragonfly. This insect works hard for its food. First, it digs a pit in sandy soil, using its tail like a shovel as it walks backward. Then it hides at the bottom of the pit. If an ant wanders too near the edge of the pit, the soft sand slides away. The ant falls in, and the ant lion has lunch.

An ant lion.

Count the legs

Animals can be grouped according to the number of legs they have. Birds have two legs. Cats, dogs, and horses have four legs. All insects have six legs. All spiders have eight. Most crustaceans, such as crabs, crayfish, and shrimp, have 6 to 14 pairs of legs. Centipedes have as many as 340 legs.

The Arthropods

- All insects are arthropods.
- Crustaceans such as lobsters, shrimp, and crabs are arthropods.
- So are arachnids (spiders, scorpions, mites, and ticks).
- Centipedes are arthropods.
- And millipedes are too.

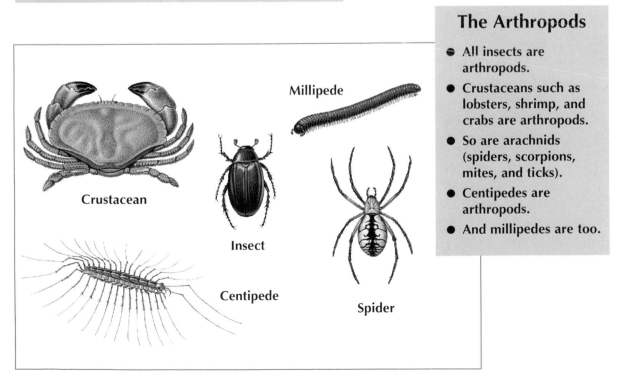

Crustacean

Millipede

Insect

Centipede

Spider

Astonishing Ants

Ants are insects that live almost everywhere on land. They like warm climates, and the only places you will not find ants are the very cold polar regions.

Some ants live in underground tunnels. Some build earth mounds. Others live inside trees or in hollow parts of plants. There are ants that build their nests from the leaves of trees. And there are some, like the army ants, which have no homes at all, and spend their lives wandering.

Big and small

Ants vary in size. Some grow to 1 inch (2.5 centimeters) long. The one above is shown life-size. It is one of the giants, named *Dinoponera grandis*. Beside its foot is a dwarf ant named *Strumigenys*. This little ant is less than 4/100 inch (0.1 centimeter) long.

The ant colony

Ants are known as "social" insects because they live in organized communities. Ants are not the only social animals in the insect world. Some kinds of bees, all termites, and some wasps also live in communities. They are social insects too.

A community of ants is called a colony. Some ant colonies are small, with as few as a dozen ants living in each one. Others have hundreds, thousands, or millions of ants living in them.

The queen and her subjects

The head of the ant colony is the queen. The queen is a special female ant. Her main job is to lay eggs. Most other members of the colony are worker ants. They are females, but they do not lay eggs. Their job is to build the nest, search for food, care for the young, and fight enemies. A few male ants live in the nest at certain times. Their only job is to mate with young queens, which will then start new colonies. Soon after mating, the male ants die.

Busy harvesters. The mounds of harvester ants are a common sight in many parts of the world. These ants collect seeds, flowers, and fruits. They store their harvest in chambers inside the nest.

Driver ants on the march. These fierce ants live in Africa.

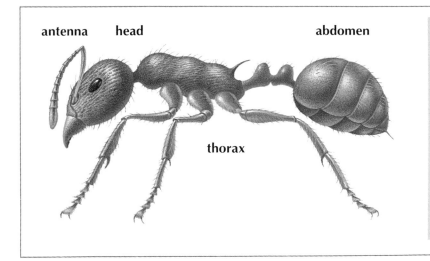

The body of an ant

Like all insects, an ant has a body with three parts. The head has eyes, two antennae, and jaws or mandibles. The middle (or thorax) has six legs. In the abdomen at the rear are the organs used to digest food and reproduce. Some ants have a sting too.

antenna   head   abdomen   thorax

Ant gardeners. These leaf-cutter ants are gardening! They bite pieces out of leaves and other plant materials, and carry the pieces to their nest. They use the leaf material to fertilize gardens of fungi inside the nest. The ants then eat parts of the fungi.

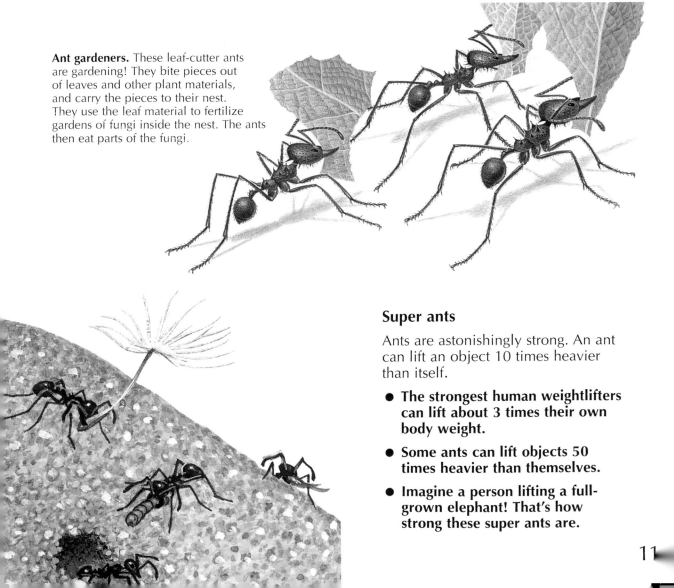

Super ants

Ants are astonishingly strong. An ant can lift an object 10 times heavier than itself.

- **The strongest human weightlifters can lift about 3 times their own body weight.**

- **Some ants can lift objects 50 times heavier than themselves.**

- **Imagine a person lifting a full-grown elephant! That's how strong these super ants are.**

Bees Are Busy

The honey store. Each cell in a honey bee hive has six sides. The bees suck up nectar from flowers. Back at the hive, they put nectar in each cell. They also add extra ingredients called enzymes. As the water in the nectar dries, the nectar changes into honey. The bees seal the cells with wax caps.

There are about 20,000 kinds of bees, and they are useful insects. They all produce honey and beeswax, but only the honey bees make enough for human use.

Bees depend on flowers for food. They collect grains of pollen and a sweet liquid called nectar from the flowers they visit. They make honey from the nectar. Bees eat honey and pollen.

How bees live

Most bees live alone, but some bees live in large groups called colonies. These bees are "social" insects, like ants. Inside each colony is a queen, along with tens of thousands of female worker bees, and a few hundred male drones.

Honey bees live in hives. The hive can be a wooden box or a hollow tree. Inside the hive, the bees build a honeycomb – a group of six-sided compartments called cells. Honeycombs are made of wax that the bees produce in their bodies.

A drone's life

Drones mate with queens. And that is all they do. They cannot feed from flowers, so they depend on workers to feed them. At the end of summer, when food becomes scarce, the workers stop feeding the drones. They drag them out of the hive to die.

Can you bee-lieve this?

- A queen bee can lay a million eggs during its five-year lifetime.

- A bee colony may contain as many as 50,000 bees.

- A worker bee has a hard life. In summer, many worker bees die exhausted after six weeks.

- Honey bees can see colors and patterns. Their eyes are sensitive to blue, yellow, and ultraviolet rays (which people cannot see).

- It isn't true that all bees sting. Some bite.

Worker   **Queen**   **Drone**

Inside a beehive. Here we can see the inside of a hive. In warm summer weather, bees have various jobs to do. On the left, nurse bees are cleaning empty cells and caring for larvae (baby bees). The big bee in the center is the queen. She is surrounded by attendants as she lays eggs, one to a cell. Worker bees collect food and defend the hive. If an enemy, such as a wasp, gets in (bottom center), the worker bees sting it to death. On the right, workers fly back to the hive carrying nectar and pollen. At the entrance to the hive (bottom right), other workers use their wings to fan in fresh air.

Solitary bees

Most kinds of bees live alone. They are solitary bees. But sometimes thousands of solitary bees gather in a small area and build their nests close together. There are no worker bees among the solitary bees. Each female is like a queen that does her own work. Carpenter bees and mason bees are solitary bees.

Carpenter bees bore tunnels in wood. The bee divides the tunnel into several cells. The cells are made of tiny wood chips stuck together with saliva. The bee puts some nectar and pollen in each cell, and then lays an egg. When the egg hatches, the larva eats the nectar and pollen. When it is ready, it chews its way out of the cell.

Mason bees build nests on walls or stones. First the bee gathers clay and moistens it with saliva to make cells that stick to the wall. Then the bee puts food in the cells, lays an egg in each, and plasters all the cells with more clay. When the clay dries, it hardens and protects the eggs. Some mason bees build nests inside empty snail shells.

Meet the Beetles . . .

Beetles make up the largest group of insects. They live everywhere. Beetles are found in rain forests and deserts, in cold places and in hot places. Some can even survive in polluted city sewers.

Beetles have a pair of front wings that are not like the wings of other insects. A beetle's wings form leathery covers that act like armor to protect the insect's body. Scientists named the beetles Coleoptera, which is Greek for "sheath wings."

Not so tough

Some beetles look fierce with their big horns and jaws. Some of these insects can bite if you disturb them. But most beetles hide or fly away when in danger.

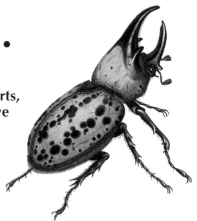

The Hercules beetle is named after a hero of ancient Greece who was famous for his strength. The Hercules beetle is a giant of the insect world. But as you can see from the life-sized picture above, it's still pretty small. Another kind of Hercules beetle lives in the West Indies and grows to twice this size. Measure the picture with a ruler, and then double the length – that's a big beetle!

Tiger beetles are hunters. The young tiger beetle lurks in a burrow and grabs passing insects to eat. Adult tiger beetles have long legs and run quickly to catch their prey with their powerful jaws. They can bite.

The ladybug has a round body. This ladybug is red with two black spots. Other kinds are yellow. Some have red, white, or yellow spots. A young ladybug looks like a miniature lizard.

The firefly or lightning bug is a beetle too. All beetles lay eggs that hatch into larvae or grubs. Most beetle grubs look like the one in the picture. As it grows, the larva sheds its tough outer covering and grows a new, larger one. The larva may do this seven times or more.

The eyed click beetle gets its name from the spots behind its head. These big "eyes" might scare off a hungry bird. It can make a sudden jump and a clicking sound by locking – and then unlocking– two segments in the middle of its body.

The larvae of click beetles look like bits of wire, and are called wireworms. Gardeners and farmers dislike wireworms because they eat the roots of plants.

4

A weevil is a beetle with a long snout. There are more than 40,000 kinds of weevils, making them the biggest beetle family. Weevils use their long snouts to bore into fruit, seeds, and other parts of plants. This boll weevil (left) is about to lunch on a cotton boll or seed pod. Once it has made a hole, it may lay eggs inside the boll. Weevil grubs (above) grow up inside the boll, chewing away.

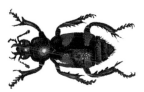

The burying beetle is also known as the sexton beetle. A sexton is a church caretaker who also digs graves, and these beetles bury small dead animals. When they find a small animal such as a mouse, the beetles dig around and under the body, until it is covered by soil. Then the female beetle lays her eggs in the mouse's body. When the eggs hatch about two weeks later, the young beetles feed on the body provided for them until they are ready to dig themselves out, and face the world.

Junebug or June beetle is a name given to several large brown beetles. Junebugs are often seen in the United States during May and June. At night, the beetles are attracted by light.

DID YOU KNOW?

- Many beetles play dead to fool a hungry bird or lizard.

- Water beetles eat snails, tadpoles, and even small fish.

- Deathwatch beetles knock their heads against the wood in which they burrow. People used to think that the ticking sound foretold a death in the house. The American drugstore beetle is also known as the deathwatch beetle.

. . . and Bugs

Many people call all insects "bugs." But true bugs are insects belonging to the group called Hemiptera.

Some bugs have wings, others do not. Unlike beetles, bugs have no chewing mouthparts. Bugs have horny snouts that look like beaks. They suck blood from animals or juices from plants.

Bugs in bed

You would not want bed bugs sleeping with you! These bugs are pests that bite people and animals, and then suck their blood. A bed bug's bite can cause your skin to swell and itch. Bed bugs are so small that they are hard to see. They hide in mattresses or between floorboards. They like warmth. In cool weather, a bed bug can go for months without feeding.

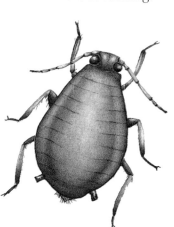

The aphid is a garden pest. These bugs make holes in plant stems and suck out the juices. Like many insects, they breed very rapidly when food is plentiful.

Growing up underground. The cicada is a bug with an unusual life story. The female cicada lays her eggs on twigs. Each egg hatches into a grub called a nymph. The nymph falls to the ground and burrows into the soil. There it stays until it is fully grown. This can take a long time. One kind of North American cicada stays underground for 17 years!

Bugs in the field. The chinch bug feeds on corn, wheat, and other grains. Adult chinch bugs hide in grass or rubbish during the winter. In spring they lay their eggs in newly planted grain fields. Young bugs eat the roots and stems of the plants. Then they crawl or fly to nearby fields of ripening grain, and lay their own eggs. Chinch bugs do great damage, especially to corn and sorghum crops.

Bugs in the water

Some bugs live in water. Among these water bugs are water striders, back swimmers, and water boatmen.
The water boatman has long, flat, back legs, covered with hairs. The bug uses these legs like oars when it swims.

The giant water bug shown here is life-size.

This bug is called a back swimmer because it swims upside down. It can stay underwater for hours. When hungry, the bug swims up beneath an unsuspecting insect on the surface and grabs it.

Phew!

Stink bugs give off an unpleasant smell when they are disturbed. This harlequin bug is a stink bug that likes to eat cabbages.

Why do people dislike some bugs?

Bugs bite and bugs can spread disease. Some are pests – they damage farm crops. Others have nasty habits.

- Assassin bugs can give a painful bite. One kind of assassin bug spits harmful saliva if you try to pick it up.
- The kissing bug usually bites people around the mouth.
- Another bug, called the bee killer, hides in flowers to attack bees.

Butterflies and Moths

Many people think that butterflies are the most beautiful of all insects. Butterflies come in every color you can imagine. They flutter from flower to flower in summer. Their beauty and grace have inspired many artists and poets.

Butterflies and moths belong to the same group of insects – Lepidoptera. The name comes from two Greek words meaning "scale wing." Powdery scales cover the wings of both butterflies and moths. Many moths are just as pretty as butterflies, but they fly at night, and so people don't often see them.

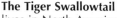

The Tiger Swallowtail lives in North America. Swallowtails are large butterflies with long tips to their back wings. These tips look like the tails of certain birds called swallows. The Queen Alexandra's birdwing is another swallowtail butterfly.

Brilliant colors

The scales on a butterfly's wings overlap. Some scales contain pigment (coloring matter). They make black, brown, red, white, and yellow colors. Other kinds of scales reflect light, like soap bubbles, and these scales produce shiny greens and blues.

The Large Skipper lives in Europe. Skippers get their name from the way they skip and dart while flying. Unlike other butterflies, skippers have plump, hairy bodies (making them more like moths). Their antennae have hooked tips, unlike the rounded antennae tips of other butterflies.

Moth

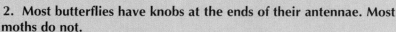

Butterfly

How to tell a butterfly from a moth

Here are four clues.

1. Most butterflies fly in the daytime. Most moths fly at night.

2. Most butterflies have knobs at the ends of their antennae. Most moths do not.

3. Most butterflies have slender, hairless bodies. Most moths have plump, furry bodies.

4. Most butterflies rest with their wings held upright. Most moths rest with their wings spread out flat.

The Western pygmy blue is one of the smallest butterflies. This tiny North American butterfly is shown here life-size.

The Sara Orangetip of North America belongs to a large worldwide family of mostly white and yellow butterflies.

The Queen Alexandra's birdwing lives in Papua New Guinea. It is the world's biggest butterfly, with wings about 11 inches (28 centimeters) across. Measure this page from top to bottom to see how big that is.

Caterpillars become butterflies

There are thousands of species, or kinds, of butterflies. All of them start life as an egg, which hatches into a caterpillar. It's hard to believe that a crawling caterpillar chewing on plants will one day turn into a gorgeous butterfly. But it does.

The Red Admiral lives in North America and Europe. It is a brush-footed butterfly. Members of this family have short front legs called brush feet. These feet are useless for walking. The butterfly brushes or scrapes plants with its feet to find out which are good to eat.

BUTTERFLY FACTS

- **The ancient Greeks believed that a person's soul left the body after death in the form of a butterfly.**

- **A butterfly cannot fly if it is too cold. It "warms up" for flying by sunning itself or shivering its wings until its flight muscles have absorbed enough heat.**

- **Butterflies have weak legs and cannot walk far.**

- **A butterfly caterpillar may eat many times its own weight in food in one day.**

The Silvery Blue butterfly lives in North America. It belongs to the largest family of butterflies, which includes blues, coppers, and hairstreaks.

The Common Australian Crow is one of the milkweed family of large, slow-flying butterflies. The North American monarch is another milkweed butterfly.

Moths

There are more than 100,000 kinds of moths, and they live all over the world. Moths have even been found on icecaps in the Arctic. Most moths fly at night.

Many moths are dull-colored. You do not notice them, especially when they are not moving. Some moths have bright spots or bands on their back wings, and a few are as colorful as butterflies.

The tiger moth has brightly colored patterns on its wings. The colors are a warning. A tiger moth caterpillar eats poisonous plants, and the poison stays in its body after it becomes a moth. A bird that eats a tiger moth gets a stomach-ache, and soon learns to avoid these bright-colored moths.

AeroBATics

Bats hunt moths at night. The bat sends out high-pitched cries. When these sounds hit a moth, their echoes guide the bat to the insect. Some kinds of moths have a special hearing organ that picks up the bat's sounds. As soon as the moth hears a bat, it tries to escape. Often it begins flying in a jerky way, like a plane doing aerobatics. This gives it a better chance of escaping the hungry bat.

A prickly mouthful. Adult moths can hide or fly away to escape enemies, but a moth caterpillar seems helpless. However, many caterpillars have sharp spines or hairs to protect them. They do not mind being seen, because their appearance acts as a "keep off" warning to hungry birds or other creatures.

The bumblebee sphinx moth looks like a bee. The moth here is feeding from a flower. The bumblebee sphinx moth has no sting, and would make a tasty meal for a bird. But most birds think that the moth is a bee, and so stay away from it.

What moths eat

Adult moths feed mainly on liquids such as nectar from flowers and fruit juices. The moth sucks up food through its proboscis (a long, hollow tongue). Moth caterpillars usually eat leaves and other parts of plants. They may also eat wood, the grubs of other insects, and clothing and other materials made of wool (sheep's hair).

The luna moth is a giant that never eats. It does not feed as an adult, so it lives only a few days. The luna moth lives in North America. It is large and colorful, with feathery antennae.

How many legs?
Caterpillars of butterflies and moths have six legs, like all insects. A caterpillar also has eight false legs, known as prolegs, in the middle of its body. At its back end it has another pair of false legs, with suckers. This arrangement of real and false legs helps the caterpillar to crawl and hang onto plants as it feeds.

The hawk moth flies fast. It beats its wings so quickly that it is often mistaken for a hummingbird.

Communication

Insects can see, hear, touch, taste, and feel. The senses of many insects are much keener than those of most other animals. Even though they cannot talk as we do, insects communicate with others of their own species.

Ants smell with their antennae. In this way, one ant can recognize another ant from the same nest. Ants drive away or kill an ant from another colony.

How insects hear

Insects communicate with one another in various ways. Many make and hear sounds, although most insects have no ears. They hear sounds by means of delicate hairs on their antennae or on other parts of their bodies. Some insects can hear sounds that are too high for human ears. Others can hear sounds that are too low for our ears to pick up.

Insect ears

A few insects do have ears, but their ears are never on their heads. Can you guess where a katydid's ears are? Look at the picture of this grasshopper on the next page, and you will be surprised.

Sounds without voices

Insects have no voices. Many make sounds by rubbing one part of their body against another part. The noisiest insects are probably grasshoppers, crickets, and cicadas. Usually only the males "sing" to attract females. Other insects, such as mosquitoes, are attracted by the beating of a female's wings. Many insects use sounds to find a mate.

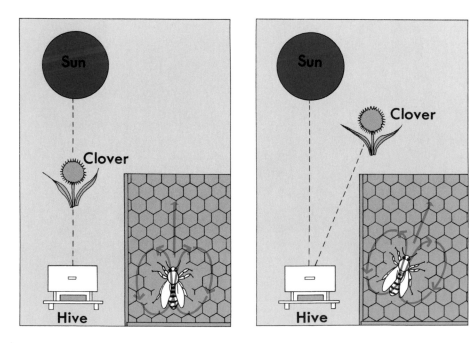

Bees dance to show other bees where food is to be found. When a worker bee returns to the hive, it dances up the honeycomb in a figure-eight pattern. The faster it dances, the nearer the food is. The food shown here is a clover plant. The direction of the bee's dance shows other bees which way to fly, using the sun as a guide.

A katydid – a singing grasshopper. Some grasshoppers rub their wings together to make sounds. Others rub a back leg against a vein in a wing, like a violin player drawing a bow across a string. This is how the katydid sings. Its song sounds like "Katy did, Katy she did."

Look closely, can you see an egg-shaped hole below the knee of the katydid's right front leg? That's one of its ears.

Touch and taste

Insects are highly sensitive to touch. An insect's touch organs are the hairs and spines all over its body – even on its eyes. The gentlest air current moves these hairs, alerting the insect.

Some insects have an amazingly sharp sense of taste. They taste things to find out if they are good to eat. Most insects have taste organs on their mouthparts. However, ants and wasps taste by touching food with their antennae. Honey bees and butterflies taste with their feet! If they step on something tasty, they stop to eat it.

Smelling a friend

Many insects use their sense of smell to find their way around, and to find food. They smell things with their antennae. Ants and bees use their antennae to find out whether another ant or bee is a friend or a stranger.

A bug that glows

The firefly, or lightning bug, is a beetle with a glow in its tail. Males flash their tail lights on and off as a mating signal. Special organs in the insect's body produce a chemical reaction to make the light.

Males flash a signal to attract females. Females flash back to show they are willing to meet, and mate.

Sometimes a hungry female firefly of a different species flashes in answer to a male's signal. The male flies to meet her – and she eats him!

Dealing with Danger

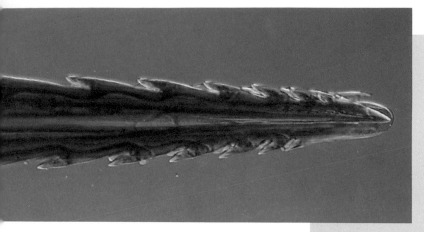

A bee's stinger

It may look like a spear, but it's really a bee's stinger magnified about 200 times.

- The stinger grows from the end of the worker bee's body. It has barbs or hooks on it.
- When the bee stings an enemy, the barbs hold tight, and the stinger is pulled out of the bee's body. Muscles inside the stinger push it deeper into the enemy, releasing poison into the wound.
- Worker bees can sting only once. They die soon afterward.
- Queen bees have smooth, curved stingers. They sting only to kill other queens, and they do not lose their stingers like worker bees.

How do insects escape their many enemies? Larger animals such as birds and reptiles eat insects. Many insects eat other insects. It's a dangerous world. Some insects have weapons to help them fool or escape their enemies. Others have developed smart tricks to make a getaway.

Most insects can sense an enemy in time to run or fly away. If you try to swat a fly, the fly takes off before your hand gets close. Tiny hairs on the fly's body detect movements in the air made by your hand.

Insect weapons

Bombardier beetles and earwigs are among the insects that use a harmful spray against their enemies. Stinkbugs, lacewings, and carrion beetles give off a foul smell. Some ants, stag beetles, and other insects nip with their jaws – hard enough to hurt a bigger animal. Bees, wasps, and some ants have poisonous stings. And other insects, including some butterflies and moths, taste so awful that they are just not worth eating.

Warning: do not touch! Stay away from hairy caterpillars. Some caterpillars have hollow hairs filled with poison. The hairs are so fine that they break at the slightest touch. This saddleback caterpillar looks like a walking cactus. Any animal getting too close is pricked by the spiky hairs. The hairs break when they pierce the animal's skin, releasing a poison.

Chemical weapons. The bombardier beetle defends itself by squirting a spray of gas. The spray is hot and irritating. The beetle has two organs at the end of its body that mix chemicals to make the spray. Earwigs, roaches, and many other insects also use chemical weapons.

A pair of startling eyes. Some moths have markings called "eye-spots." The spots look like eyes on their wings. They fool an inquisitive bird into thinking the moth is too big to eat. Suddenly seeing the spots can startle an enemy long enough for the moth to escape.

25

Egg to Adult

Most insects have short lives. They quickly become adults and reproduce. Their eggs hatch and grow into new adults in a few weeks, so many insects produce several generations in a season.

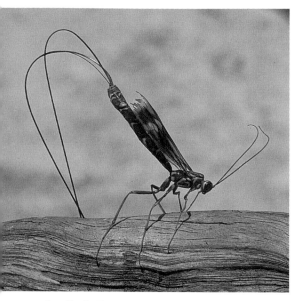

Most insects lay eggs but some, such as cockroaches, flies, and beetles, give birth to living young. As a rule, insects do not take care of their young. After the male and female mate, the female lays the eggs, and leaves them. When the eggs hatch, the young insects must take care of themselves.

Good parents

The earwig is one of the few insects that cares for its young. Earwigs keep their eggs clean, guard them until the young hatch, and then watch over the young. A few kinds of beetles also stay with their young after they are born, guarding and feeding them.

The earwig is a watchful parent.

A deadly drill. The ichneumon wasp makes sure its young have a food supply. The female drives its long egg-laying organ (called an ovipositor) into a tree, seeking the grubs of other insects. When the wasp finds a grub, it lays an egg in the grub's body. The ichneumon larva hatches inside the grub, and feeds off the grub's fat.

THE FACTS OF LIFE

In some insect species, males are extremely rare or even unknown. Female aphids can reproduce without the aid of a male at all.

A queen honey bee needs just one mating period. After that, she can lay hundreds of eggs a day for the rest of her life. She is the mother of all the thousands of bees in the hive.

A cicada emerges from its nymph skin to become an adult insect, with wings. As a nymph, it sheds its skin several times, and leaves its last skin hanging from a plant.

egg

From egg to butterfly

The female butterfly lays eggs on a plant that the young will be able to eat. The eggs are stuck onto the plant by a sticky substance. Out of the egg crawls a caterpillar. First it eats its own eggshell, and then it starts eating the plant leaves. It grows rapidly. When fully grown, the caterpillar forms a hard shell called a pupa. Inside the shell an amazing change takes place. When the shell splits open, out comes a butterfly. In an hour or so the butterfly is ready to fly away. It finds a mate, and the cycle starts all over again.

young caterpillar

butterfly

pupa

fully grown caterpillar

nymph

dragonfly

Metamorphosis

Only a few insects, such as silverfish, look like miniatures of their parents when they hatch. A dragonfly comes out of its egg as a nymph – an ugly creature with no wings that lives in water. A butterfly comes out of its egg as a caterpillar. It has to go through another stage, as a pupa, before it can become an adult. This change of form is called *metamorphosis*.

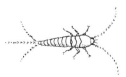

silverfish

Feeding and Food

Insects can eat all kinds of food. Many eat plants. Some eat other insects. Insects eat fabrics, cork, paste, and even face powder! Because they are so small, many insects don't need much food. A crumb is a banquet for an insect.

Probably the greediest insects are caterpillars. They hardly ever stop eating. They gobble away at plants until they reach full size. When a caterpillar becomes a butterfly, it eats different foods. A butterfly has no chewing mouthparts for eating leaves. It uses its tubelike proboscis to suck up nectar from flowers. Most butterflies feed only on nectar. Some butterflies do not feed at all.

Army ants are fierce insects, with powerful jaws. A grasshopper caught by the ants is quickly torn to bits.

Crop-munchers

Plant-eating insects can harm the plants they feed on. The damage is worse when thousands or even millions of insects arrive at the same time. A swarm of locusts can destroy entire fields of farm crops.

A copper butterfly feeding on nectar from a flower. Its long sucking tube, or proboscis, coils up when not in use.

Hunters

Some insects are hunters that prey on other insects. Army ants travel in huge numbers. The army will surround and attack small creatures such as mice and lizards, or any animal that cannot escape quickly.

Food gatherers

Ants and bees collect food and take it back to their nests. A few other insects also collect food. Dung beetles, for instance, roll balls of animal dung to their burrows. The female beetle lays her eggs in the dungball, which provides food for the young beetles after they hatch.

Locusts eating the leaves of corn plants. When a locust chews, its jaws move sideways, not up and down as ours do.

A scarab beetle pulling a dungball.

Food fit for a queen

Baby bees are fed by "nurse" bees on royal jelly, a creamy food that is rich in vitamins and proteins. Worker bees produce the food in their bodies.

- After three days, the nurse bees switch to feeding the babies on bee bread, a mixture of honey and pollen.
- Sometimes a few chosen babies are fed only on royal jelly. These babies grow up to be new queens.

A caterpillar may eat many times its own weight of leaves in one day.

Of all the insects, ants have some of the most amazing ways of finding and storing food. There are harvesters, farmers, and living honeypots!

Harvesters

Harvester ants collect seeds and store them in special chambers inside their nests. They tear off the tough husks of the seeds and chew the kernels (the insides) into a soft pulp called ant bread. Then they squeeze out the liquid and swallow it.

Dairy farmers

Other ants are dairy farmers. They live mainly on a sugary liquid called honeydew. They get the honeydew from other insects, mostly from aphids and other plant lice. Plant lice suck juices from plants. The juices contain more sugar and water than the lice need, so they get rid of the excess as honeydew. Dairying ants visit the plants on which aphids feed. When an ant strokes an aphid with its antennae, the aphid releases a drop of honeydew, and the ant licks up the sugary food.

Dairy-farmer ants take care of their "herds." They protect the aphids, and drive off other insects. Some ants carry their plant lice into the warmth of the ant nest in winter. Others keep herds of plant lice on roots inside the ant nest. When a young queen ant leaves the nest to start a new ant colony, she carries an egg-laying plant louse with her to start a new dairy herd.

Dairy-farmer ants. The yellow insects shown are aphids. When the ants stroke them with their antennae, the aphids release drops of honeydew. The ants eat the sugary liquid.

Harvester ants store seeds in special chambers inside their nests.

PARTNERS

Some kinds of ants have a special relationship with certain kinds of plants.

- Plant ants are attracted to a particular kind of plant by a special food that the plant grows for the ants to eat.
- In return for a home and food, the ants protect the plant. They drive off leaf-eating insects. They will even sting a sheep or a deer that tries to eat the leaves of their plant.
- Scientists call this kind of partnership *symbiosis*. Both partners – the plant and the ants – benefit from the arrangement.

Living honeypots

Honeypot ants gather honeydew from insects, or from plants. Inside their nests, these ants have living food stores. Certain worker ants are fed with honeydew until their bodies swell like balloons. They become living honeypots, so fat that they cannot walk. They hang from the roof of a chamber inside the ant nest.

When a nestmate is hungry, it goes to the storage chamber and taps a honeypot with its antennae. The honeypot brings up some honeydew from its stomach, and the hungry ant eats.

Honeypot ants. These living storage tanks just hang around, waiting for nestmates to come for a snack.

Flies

The Mediterranean fruit fly lays its eggs in fruit. It is a harmful pest.

Flies buzz around food in the kitchen. A fly that lands on a table probably carries germs inside its body. When it touches food, it leaves some germs behind. Flies carry germs that cause diseases in animals and people.

There are about 100,000 kinds of flies, but not all flies are pests. Some kinds of flies are helpful. They carry pollen from one plant to another. Other flies eat harmful insects. Scientists use fruit flies in the study of heredity. These flies provide valuable information on how characteristics are passed on from one generation to the next.

Two wings

All true flies have two wings. Some other insects are called flies – such as butterflies and dragonflies. But these insects have four wings. They are not true flies.

Fancy fliers

Flies fly in a remarkable way. They do not need to run or jump to get into the air. As soon as a fly beats its wings, it's flying. The wings keep on beating until the fly's feet touch something to land on. Instead of back wings, a fly has rodlike parts called halteres that vibrate in time with the beat of the fly's wings. The halteres balance the insect as it flies and help it dart quickly in any direction.

A house fly's meal. A house fly on a crust of bread, like this one, is not about to bite off a crumb to eat. A house fly does not bite or chew food, because it cannot open its jaws. It can eat only liquids. So the fly makes dry food moist by spitting on it. Then it uses two soft mouthparts like sponges to lap up the liquid. Flies do not have very tidy table manners!

FLY FACTS

- **The buzzing of a fly is the sound of its wings beating.**
- **A house fly beats its wings about 200 times a second.**
- **A mosquito's wings beat about 1,000 times a second.**

What a fly sees

A fly is always on the watch for danger and for food. These insects have large eyes. A house fly has about 4,000 lenses in each eye. Each lens gives the insect a slightly different picture. Everything a fly sees seems to be broken up into small bits. A fly does not see you clearly, but it sees your slightest movement.

The greenbottle is a fly with a shiny green coat.

How long does a house fly live? About 21 days in summer, and longer in cool weather when flies are less active.

What happens to flies in winter? Most adult flies die. Some hibernate. Many larvae and pupae live through the winter and develop into adults in spring.

A mosquito. The name mosquito means "little fly" in Spanish. Mosquitoes lay their eggs in or near water. Only female mosquitoes "bite", and only a few kinds attack people and animals to sip their blood.

The house fly's life cycle

Like other insects, flies lay eggs. House flies lay their eggs in dung or food waste. Each egg hatches into a wriggling larva, which is called a maggot. The maggot eats and grows, and then becomes a pupa. The adult fly forms inside the pupa.

eggs

maggots

pupa

adult fly

Going Places

Some caterpillars move in very odd ways. The measuring worm caterpillar crawls by arching its body in loops.

Insects can walk, climb, and fly. Some insects swim, others burrow. Each insect's body is adapted for it to go to the kinds of places where it will find food and reproduce.

How insects walk

An insect's leg has not one but FOUR knees! The middle section of an insect's body, called the thorax, is in three parts or segments. One pair of legs is connected to each segment. Each leg has five main segments, with movable joints or "knees" between them.

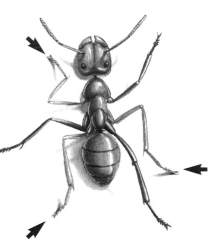

When an insect walks, it always keeps three of its six legs on the ground.

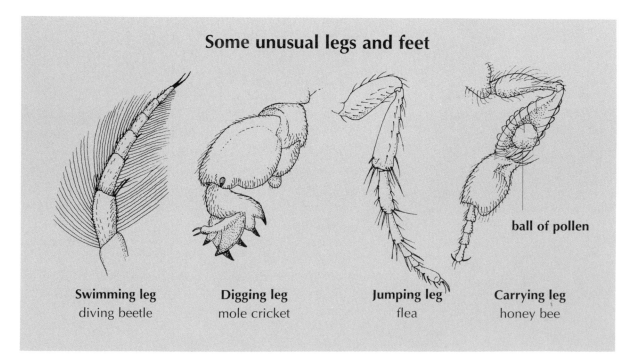

Some unusual legs and feet

Swimming leg
diving beetle

Digging leg
mole cricket

Jumping leg
flea

Carrying leg
honey bee

ball of pollen

Steady on their feet

When we walk, we balance ourselves on one leg as we step forward with the other. When insects walk, they usually move the middle leg on one side along with the front and hind legs on the other side. The insect always has three legs on the ground to support its body and keep it steady.

Dragonflies have four large wings. Most kinds of insects have one or two pairs of wings, as well as six legs.

Swimmers

Some insects prefer life in the water. They use their legs for swimming. Hairs on their legs make them work better as paddles.

Diggers

Mole crickets and dung beetles use their broad front legs like shovels for digging in the soil.

Jumpers and carriers

Locusts, fleas, and grasshoppers use their long, muscular hind legs for jumping.
Honey bees have pollen-collecting brushes on their front legs, and baskets for carrying pollen on their hind legs.

How can a house fly walk upside down?

Flies have claws on their feet that help them cling to walls and ceilings. House flies also have hairy pads on their feet. A sticky substance on the feet helps the insects walk on smooth, slippery windows.

Flying

Flying insects use two sets of muscles to beat their wings. One set of muscles makes the wings move up, the other set makes the wings move down. Other muscles at the base of the wings control the direction of flight. Many insects can hover like a helicopter – or even fly backward.

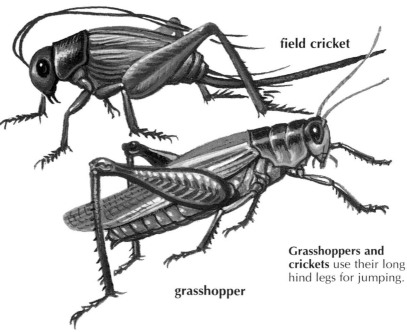

field cricket

Grasshoppers and crickets use their long hind legs for jumping.

grasshopper

Hide-and-Seek

Many insects are hard to see.
Some look like sticks, green leaves, dry leaves, or snail shells. Others look like thorns, dry reeds, or bird droppings. Some are so well disguised that you need to get really close to see them at all. They play hide-and-seek to fool their enemies.

Protective coloration

Many insects escape from their enemies because their color or form blends with their surroundings. When they are resting on tree trunks, many moths look like bark or bird droppings. This form of camouflage is called protective coloration.

Protective resemblance

Walkingsticks or stick insects look like twigs. Even when they move, it is hard to spot them. Some caterpillars look like twigs too. Leafhoppers look like the thorns and spines of plants. This form of protection is called protective resemblance. Insects that look like twigs or leaves have a good chance of escaping an enemy.

Which is the twig and which is the insect? The walkingstick's long, thin body and sticklike legs make it very hard to see.

Is it a thorn or an insect? Can you see a treehopper on the stem of this rosebush? It looks so much like a thorn that birds often overlook the insect.

A moth is resting on this tree bark. When it keeps still, the moth seems to disappear – its coloring blends with the bark on the tree. The same moth resting on a flower or green grass would be seen much more easily.

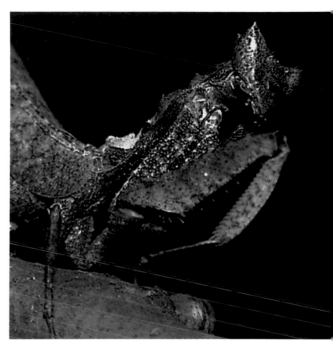

Beware this leaf!

Disguise can also aid an insect looking for its next meal. The praying mantis has a long body and broad, leaflike wings. It looks like a torn leaf when it stands still. If another insect comes close, the mantis grabs it.

The wings of the dead-leaf mantis may look like leaves, but any small insect wandering near the mantis had better watch out.

The inchworm is the caterpillar of a moth. A bird can mistake it for a twig, unless it looks very closely. The caterpillar can hold itself so stiff that it looks just like part of the tree.

Homes

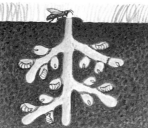

Underground apartments. The mining bee burrows into loose soil to make a tunnel nest. Although these bees are solitary insects, many mining bees share the same main tunnel leading to the surface. However, each bee has its own apartment underground.

Most insects have no homes. They do not make homes for themselves, like many mammals do. They do not make nests for their young, like most birds do. A few kinds of insects live in large groups called colonies. They build homes with many rooms and connecting passages.

Diggers, carpenters, and weavers

Ants are called "social insects" because they live in colonies. Many ants share a nest. Ants build many types of nests. Most make their homes underground, carving out chambers and tunnels in the soil. Some build mounds of soil, twigs, and pine needles over their nests. Inside are tunnels that lead to nurseries for young ants, as well as storerooms and special rooms for use in cold or rainy weather.

Carpenter ants chew tunnels in wood. Tropical weaver ants make nests from tree leaves. To make a nest, some workers hold the edges of the leaves together, while others carry silk-spinning ant larvae backward and forward across the edges. The larvae make a sheet of silken webbing that binds the leaves together.

Bees and wasps

Bees and wasps are also talented nest-builders. Bees make hives of wax with many compartments or cells that they use for various purposes. Some cells serve as nurseries for young bees. Others are used to store food.

Some wasps build many-celled nests out of paper. Others dig nesting burrows in the ground. Some wasps take over burrows abandoned by beetles. They make separate rooms for each young wasp, using bits of grass, stone, or mud. Daubers and potter wasps make nests out of mud.

A hornets' nest. Hornets are wasps that build large paper nests out of chewed-up wood and plant material. Wasps often hang their nests from trees, but they also nest in burrows once occupied by rodents, or even in buildings.

Mound-builders

Termites are insects that thrive in warm climates. Some termites mix soil with saliva to make a kind of cement. They build huge mound-nests. These nests may be as high as three men standing on one another's shoulders! Termites avoid sunlight, and build underground tunnels to find food. Inside the termite mound are numerous chambers and galleries. The termite king and queen live in the center of the nest.

Winter camp for caterpillars. At the end of summer, caterpillars of the brown-tail moth spin sturdy tents of silk in the branches of trees. Then they spend the winter snug inside the tent.

The leaf-roller beetle uses leaves as egg-holders. The female leaf-roller first makes cuts in a leaf, then rolls it up, and lays eggs in the folds.

Look inside a harvester ant nest. The large queen has her own special chamber. In the nurseries, worker ants take care of the eggs and larvae. Seeds collected by the workers are brought to the storerooms. Other worker ants dig out new rooms. In winter the ants cluster in the deepest rooms for warmth.

Amazing ants' nests

- Some ants' nests have as few as 12 ants living in them.

- Other nests may be home to as many as 10 million ants.

- The biggest ants' nests are mounds linked by underground tunnels. They may be as big as a tennis court.

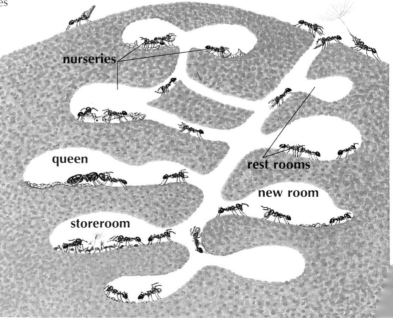

nurseries

queen

rest rooms

new room

storeroom

Insects and Flowers

Insects need flowers, but flowers also need insects. Many insects depend on flowers for food, and many flowers rely on insects for pollination. Insects carry the yellow pollen dust that fertilizes the female parts of flowers so that they can produce seeds.

How bees see flowers. This picture shows how we see yellow flowers (left). When photographed in ultraviolet light (right), the same flowers appear as a bee sees them. The dark areas are target zones, where the insect will find nectar and pollen.

Bees, butterflies, and some beetles and flies feed on nectar. They find this liquid food in flowers. When an insect lands on a flower in search of food, pollen grains from the flower stick to its body. Then, when the insect visits other flowers, some of these pollen grains brush off onto these flowers. In this way, flowers of the same kind exchange pollen and are able to make seed to reproduce themselves. Apples, plums, oranges, and grapes are among the many fruits that also depend on insects for pollination.

Attracting insects

Most of the flowers that depend on insects for pollination are brightly colored or heavily scented. Different insects are attracted by different colors and scents. Some insects pollinate only one kind of flower. The red clover, for example, is pollinated by bumblebees. But the bumblebee does not see this flower as we do, because bees cannot see red.

Bees are strongly attracted by yellow and blue flowers. Unlike people, bees can see ultraviolet light. Many flowers, particularly yellow ones, have ultraviolet markings, and these markings attract bees.

The yucca moth

The yucca flowers of the Southwestern United States are pollinated only by the yucca moth.

- The female moth carries pollen from one yucca plant to a flower on a second yucca plant.

- The moth lays its eggs in the second flower and then deposits pollen from the first flower onto the seed-making parts of the second flower.

- The moth eggs and the yucca seeds develop together.

- The eggs hatch into caterpillars, which feed on the seeds. But enough seeds remain to grow into new yucca plants.

Night scents

Many flowers that attract moths open only at night, when many of the insects search for food. These flowers are usually pale or white, so they are easier to see in the darkness. They also give off heavy scents that attract moths and other night-flying insects.

Beetles also pollinate flowers. These insects prefer white or pale flowers with spicy scents – such as magnolias or wild roses.

Flies do not have the long sucking mouthparts needed to drink nectar from deep inside tube-shaped flowers. For this reason, they like flat flowers such as buttercups. Flies are also drawn to certain flowers that give off a foul smell like rotting food.

A bee's hairy body becomes covered with pollen dust as it flies from flower to flower.

Collecting pollen

Many flowers make sure that visiting insects bring pollen from other flowers, and take away new pollen. For example, to reach the nectar in a snapdragon flower, a bee has to push its way inside. In doing so, it brushes off pollen dust it has picked up from other flowers. Then, as it scrambles out, the bee is covered with a dusting of the flower's own pollen. It carries this pollen away to other flowers.

A butterfly rests on a flower. Butterflies use their long mouthparts to reach into the flower and suck up nectar. Like bees, butterflies prefer flowers with sweet-smelling yellow or blue blossoms.

Lookalikes

Some insects mimic, or look like, another insect. Why should this be? A harmless insect usually mimics another insect that has powerful weapons or that tastes bad. Being a mimic gives helpless insects a way to protect themselves.

Bad taste

Birds leave the monarch butterfly alone because they don't like its taste. The monarch's bright colors advertise the fact that it tastes bad. Another kind of butterfly, called the viceroy, is an insect that tastes good to a bird. However, few birds try eating this butterfly. The viceroy looks like a monarch butterfly, so birds leave it alone because they think it will taste bad. The viceroy has the same warning colors as the monarch and being a lookalike gives this insect a better chance of living a little longer.

Monarch butterfly

Keep off!

You notice a wasp as soon as it lands near you. Insects that bite or sting, such as wasps and bees, usually have bright colors. It is easy for a bird or a lizard to spot these warning colors, and steer clear of the insect.

Some insects that have no protective weapons, such as stings, mimic insects that do. Robber flies look so much like bumblebees that other animals avoid them, even though the flies have no sting. There are beetles, hoverflies, and drone flies that also look like bees or wasps.

Can you spot the difference? The insect on the left is a robber fly. The insect on the right is a bee. Because the fly looks like a bee, it is left alone by hungry enemies.

Wasps sting. By looking like a wasp, this stingless fly (left) is less likely to be eaten than other flies. Birds mistake it for a wasp (right).

Sting or no sting?

Most animals hesitate if they see a black and yellow wasp. The wasp's bold stripes warn other animals that it will sting if attacked. Look at the insects pictured above. The one on the right is a wasp. The one on the left is a syrphid fly. The fly has no sting. But it looks so like a wasp that birds choose to look for a meal elsewhere.

Lookalike killers

Being a lookalike can also help a hunter. Assassin bugs mimic the kind of insect that they prey on. One kind of assassin bug looks just like a walkingstick. Another could pass for a mosquito. There is even an assassin bug that looks like a praying mantis. This mimicry helps the assassin bug come close to its prey without being recognized. By the time the victim realizes its mistake, it's usually too late.

An ant or not?

Is this an ant or a lookalike ant? It has an ant's body – but count the legs. Right! This animal has eight legs. It is not an ant, and not even an insect. It is an antlike spider – a spider that deceives its prey by looking like an ant.

The antlike spider is a spider that mimics an ant. Its body shape is more like an ant's than a spider's.

Mass Movements

Some insects travel in large numbers and across long distances. These mass movements are called migrations. Despite their small size, some insects fly across mountains and oceans during these seasonal journeys.

Butterflies on the move

Every autumn, North American monarch butterflies gather in great clouds. They fly south to spend the winter in warmer tropical or subtropical areas. In spring, the butterflies drift northward again, laying eggs as they go. Few monarchs live long enough to complete the return trip. Their offspring, after becoming adults, continue the northward journey. Monarchs may migrate from as far north as Canada to California or Florida in the United States, or to Mexico.

Other butterflies that migrate include the painted lady and the red admiral, which fly between Europe and North Africa.

Monarch butterflies huddle together. The insects are resting on a branch of a tree after their long flight.

Locusts by the million

Many other insects make long migratory flights. The locusts are probably the best known. Locusts often travel in swarms so huge that they block out the sun.

Scientists do not know why locusts migrate. These insects live in hot countries, so they do not need to fly to warmer areas for the winter. And they do not migrate because they are hungry, either. In fact, locusts may leave a land where food is plentiful and not stop to feed during most of their long flight. The signal for the mass flight seems to be the build-up of an enormous population. A swarm of migrating locusts may number in the billions. Wherever they settle down, they destroy every bit of plant life.

Swarming desert locusts cover this truck in Africa. The sky is full of flying insects. A locust swarm may devour food crops and leave farms in ruin.

Hibernation

Many insects die when winter approaches, but many others live through the cold by hibernating. Some hibernate as eggs or larvae, some as adults. They spend the winter in barns, cellars, attics, caves, holes in trees, burrows in the ground, or other places that are sheltered from the winter weather. You may even find insects hibernating in your house. Insects that can survive the winter include house flies, mosquitoes, ladybugs, and some moths and butterflies.

A swarm of bees hangs from a tree branch. Thousands of bees cluster together, while scout bees search for a site for a new hive.

Why bees swarm

Bees swarm when their colony becomes overcrowded. The queen bee lays eggs from which new queens will hatch before she and many of the worker bees leave the nest. Some workers stay behind to care for the new queen, who must first kill all her rivals. The swarming bees fly away and cling together in a large mass, while scouts look for a site to start a new nest.

Ladybugs cluster together for warmth during the winter. These beetles migrate from their summer feeding grounds to sheltered places, where they hibernate in great masses.

Pests and Parasites

All insects have their place in the great web of life that includes human beings and every other living thing. Insects feed on plants and animals. Some are regarded as pests because they damage crops, food, and houses, or carry diseases.

A German cockroach and nymph. Cockroaches eat or spoil food in homes, stores, restaurants, and bakeries.

Only a small number of insects are harmful, however. Farmers dislike insects that eat valuable farm crops. These pests include the boll weevil, which damages cotton plants; the Hessian fly, which attacks wheat; and the Colorado beetle, which feeds on potatoes.

Butterflies can be pests too. The caterpillar of the cabbage white butterfly eats the leaves of cabbages, cauliflowers, and related food crops.

Household pests

Many insects are household pests. Clothes moths damage clothing, and carpet beetles damage carpets and upholstery. Silverfish damage books, and termites chew through furniture and wood in buildings. Cockroaches eat or spoil food in homes, restaurants, and warehouses.

Disease carriers

The worst insect enemies are those that damage our health by carrying diseases. Bloodsucking insects carry such deadly diseases as malaria and sleeping sickness.

Controlling insect pests

Harmful insects, such as disease-carrying mosquitoes, can be kept down by draining the swamps where they breed, and destroying their eggs. Insect pests often travel from country to country.

The Colorado beetle lays its eggs on potato plants. Both the adult beetles and the larvae feed on the leaves of the plants.

Fleas

Fleas are small, wingless insects. They live on the skin of mammals and birds, sucking blood for food. Fleas can be dangerous pests because they can carry the germs that cause diseases such as bubonic plague and typhus.

- **Fleas are called parasites because they live on other creatures, including people. Instead of finding their own food, fleas puncture the skin of their "host" with their beaks to get blood.**

- **When their host dies, fleas leave at once to find a new host, because they must have blood for food.**

- **The common human flea lives in the folds of clothing, and drops its eggs around the house. The larvae look like maggots. When they become adults, they jump onto a person.**

The screwworm fly lays its eggs in sores on farm animals. The maggots eat into the flesh, often killing the animal. Scientists used "biological control" methods to combat the screwworm. They sterilized male flies so that the insects could not reproduce.

Insect pests hide in cargoes of food or timber on ships and planes. Government officials inspect cargoes at ports and airports to search for these unwanted insect stowaways.

Sometimes a predator that eats the pest can help solve a pest problem. In California, an Australian scale insect almost destroyed the lemon and orange groves. Then the fruit growers brought in ladybugs. The ladybugs ate the scale insects, and saved the fruit crop.

The Japanese beetle eats the leaves and fruits of about 275 kinds of plants! Its larvae eat the roots.

The European bark beetle is one of two kinds of bark beetles that spread Dutch elm fungus disease. The disease kills elm trees.

Poisonous chemicals or insecticides can be used to kill insect pests. But most of these chemicals also kill harmless insects and other animals. Using such chemicals can upset the balance of nature. Scientists are looking for better methods of controlling insect pests.

The wireworm is the larva of the click beetle. It lives underground, eating the roots of plants.

Prehistoric Insects

The ancient ancestors of insects were creatures that crawled and swam in the prehistoric oceans.

An ant trapped in amber – a sticky resin that oozed from pine trees in prehistoric times. When the resin hardened, the ant's body was preserved inside the amber. This ant is about 30 million years old.

Moving onto dry land

Insects first appeared on the earth at least 400 million years ago. Most experts believe that the ancestors of insects were wormlike animals that lived in the sea. At that time, all animals lived in the sea. Plants first grew on dry land about 430 million years ago. Plants provided food for animals that moved onto the land from the ocean. Primitive forms of insects and spiders were among the first animals to make their homes on dry land.

Giants of the forest

Insects flew among the strange plants of the huge swampy forests that grew on the land. Some prehistoric insects were larger than the insects we see today. There were dragonflies as big as crows, and giant cockroaches nearly as long as a pencil. Insects lived all over the earth during the age of dinosaurs and the later age of mammals. Insects became the most numerous animals on our planet.

Fossil remains show that some insects have not changed in millions of years. This dragonfly lived about 150 million years ago.

Useful and Unusual Insects

We think of some insects as useful and others as harmful, but all insects are useful in some way. They are an important part of the balance of nature. Without them, life as we know it would not exist.

Food for others

Insects are an important food source for birds, fish, frogs, lizards, and many small mammals. Insects even serve as food for a few plants, such as the Venus's flytrap, pitcher plant, and sundew.

Insect products

Insects provide us with various useful products. Honey and beeswax are made by bees. Silk moth caterpillars, known as silkworms, produce silk. Shellac, a varnish, comes from lac, a sticky substance produced by a scale insect. Cochineal, a dye, comes from the cochineal scale insect.

Beekeepers keep bees in hives. The bees build their honeycombs in drawerlike sections that can be taken out of the hive. These beekeepers wear veils to protect their faces from bee stings. A few experienced beekeepers handle bees and honeycombs with their bare hands.

Farmers' friends

Farmers need insects because bees, wasps, flies, butterflies, and other insects pollinate plants. Many fruits depend on insects to spread their pollen. Without the insects' help, these plants would not make seeds. Peas, onions, carrots, cabbages, and clover also depend on insects for pollination. So do many garden flowers.

Waste removers

Many insects help keep the world clean. They are waste removers, feeding on animal wastes, including dung, and the bodies of dead animals.

Gardeners welcome ladybugs. These beetles are useful because they eat aphids, pests that suck the juices of many plants. This ladybug is enjoying a meal, and ridding the plant of unwanted visitors at the same time.

Pest controllers

Some insects eat harmful pests. The ladybug, for example, eats aphids. Other insects are parasites that live in or on the bodies of harmful insects. Some wasps lay their eggs on caterpillars that damage tomato plants. As the young wasps develop, they feed on the caterpillars and kill them.

A silkworm moth and (top) a silkworm making a cocoon. The large white silk moth lays eggs that hatch into caterpillars called silkworms. When the caterpillar is ready to become a pupa, it spins a cocoon or outer wrapping of fine silk. According to ancient legend, the wife of a Chinese emperor discovered silk about 4,700 years ago. Today, cultivated silk is spun by silkworms raised on silk farms.

Insects have an amazing variety of shapes and ways of life. Some are so tiny that they live between the thin walls of a leaf. The young of some insects live in pools of crude oil! Let's meet some unusual members of the insect community.

A praying mantis. These insects look like the plants on which they lie in wait for their victims.

An insect that eats frogs

The mantis is sometimes called the praying mantis, because it holds up its front legs as if it were praying. Mantises eat other insects – including other mantises. They even eat small tree frogs. The mantis uses its armlike front legs to grasp its prey. These legs have sharp spines and hooks that hold the insect's captives.

An insect that rarely moves

The scale insect does not look like most other insects. It gets its name from the waxy or scaly shell that usually covers its body. Some scale insects have no eyes, no feelers, and no legs. They cluster on plants and rarely move. Another odd fact is that the adult male scale insect has no mouth and cannot feed. It lives just long enough to fertilize the female's eggs.

whirligig beetles

large diving beetle

giant scavenger beetle

Some insects swim and dive. Whirligigs are water beetles that whirl on top of pools. Diving beetles and giant scavenger beetles hunt beneath the surface. They feed on small fish and insect larvae.

The scale insect looks like a shell.

Insects on the menu

Some people eat insects. In South Africa, some people roast termites and eat them by the handful, like popcorn.

● **Mexicans make a cake out of the eggs of water boatmen.**

● **In the United States, some stores sell fried caterpillars and chocolate-covered bees and ants.**

● **Australian aborigines traditionally ate insect grubs, which are rich in fats and sugars. They particularly enjoyed witchetty grubs, a kind of beetle larvae. Toasted lightly, the grubs taste somewhat like scrambled eggs.**

Wasps that paralyze

Some female wasps will attack a spider larger than themselves in order to lay an egg on the spider's body. The wasp fights the spider, and turns it onto its back. Then the wasp plunges its poisonous sting into the spider's soft underside. The poison paralyzes the spider. The wasp then drags its helpless captive to its nest and lays an egg on it.

Other wasps lay their eggs on caterpillars. They do this so that their young will have a supply of fresh food. The wasp does all this by instinct, without having to learn how. A young insect is not taught by its parents. Its patterns of behavior are inherited.

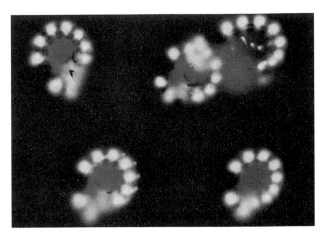

Some insects glow in the dark. These larvae of a South American beetle look like neon lights. They are called railroad worms.

A life and death battle. The tarantula hawk wasp (right) is a female, about to fight a tarantula spider. If the wasp wins the battle, the spider is doomed to provide food for the wasp's young.

51

Spiders

Spiders live in the same kinds of places as insects. Some people are afraid of spiders. Many others find them fascinating. Spiders are best known for the silk webs they spin. All spiders spin silk, but not all spiders make webs.

The female black widow of North America is one of the few spiders dangerous to humans. The bite of a female black widow can cause illness and severe pain. Some people have died after a black widow bite, but the deaths usually resulted from complications, and not from the bite itself.

Spiders everywhere

More than 30,000 kinds of spiders are known to us today but scientists believe there may be as many as 50,000 to 100,000 kinds. Spiders live anywhere they can find food. They can be seen in fields, woods, swamps, caves, and deserts. They also live in houses. One kind of spider spends most of its life under water. Another kind lives near the top of Mount Everest, the world's highest mountain.

STRANGE SPIDER FACTS

- Most spiders have eight eyes. Some spiders have six, four, or two eyes, and some have no eyes at all.
- A spider has no bones. Its tough skin serves as a protective outer skeleton.
- Spiders have poison fangs for biting, but they cannot chew their food. A spider softens the solid parts of its victims by spraying digestive juice on them. It then sucks up the liquid food through a kind of built-in straw.
- Some spiders can live for a year without eating.

A trap-door spider peers out of its burrow. This spider digs a burrow in the ground and covers the entrance with a hinged door made of silk and mud. Then the spider waits. When an insect walks by, the spider opens the door, seizes and poisons its victim, and drags it into its burrow.

Dinner is served. This black-and-yellow spider makes a round silken web between tree branches or plant stems. It uses bands of silk to tie up insects caught in the web. The spider stores the insect in its silk wrappings until it is ready to dine.

The triangle spider spins a triangle-shaped web between two twigs. The small drawing shows this spider's actual size. Other spiders pictured on these and following pages are shown larger than life.

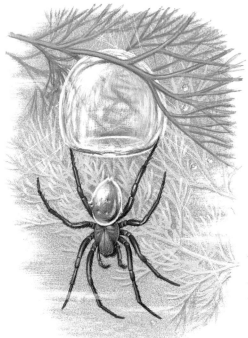

Spiders are hunters

All spiders hunt animals for food. They catch insects and other small animals. All spiders have biting fangs, and most kinds of spiders can give a poisonous bite. A spider's bite kills its victims, such as a fly caught in its web. A few kinds of spiders have a bite that can harm people. Many spiders trap their prey, like the familiar garden spider patiently spinning its web, and the trap-door spider, waiting behind the door of its burrow. Others run swiftly to catch their victims, and some even hunt underwater.

The water spider is an underwater diver that lives in Europe and parts of Asia. It makes an airtight nest of silk, shaped like a bell. The spider fills the silken bell with air bubbles that it holds close to its body. It can live on this air supply for several months.

Amazing silk-spinners

Spider silk is the strongest natural fiber known. It is made by special glands in the spider's body. Some glands make a liquid silk that dries outside the body, while other glands make a silk that stays sticky.

Spiders spin silk with short, fingerlike organs called spinnerets. Using different spinnerets, a spider can mix silk from different silk glands to make a very thin thread or a thick band of silk. Some spiders make beaded threads to help trap jumping or flying insects. Others spin very thin threads of extremely sticky silk. The spider weaves sticky threads and dry threads into a ribbonlike thread called a hackled band. It uses this band to catch and tie up its prey.

A garden spider on its web. This spider is one of the kinds known as orb weaver spiders.

Orb weavers spin big, round webs

- The threads running out from the center of the web look like the spokes of a wheel. These threads are made of dry silk.

- Threads of sticky silk connect the spokes.

- The sticky threads trap any insect that flies or falls into the web.

- An orb weaver often spins a new web every night.

- The spider eats the old web. This way, it reuses the silk, and eats any tiny insects it might have missed.

Ogre-faced stick spider

Some spiders hunt with nets

- The ogre-faced stick spider holds its web in its front legs.

- The web is about the size of a postage stamp.

- When it spots an insect, the spider stretches the web to several times normal size.

- Then it sweeps the net over its prey.

54

Swinging on a thread

Spiders depend on silk in so many ways that they could not live without it. Wherever a spider goes, it drags a silk thread behind it. This thread, called a dragline, can help the spider escape from its enemies. If a hungry bird comes too near its web, the spider can use its dragline to drop from the web to the ground, or hang in the air. When the danger is past, the spider climbs back up the dragline to its web. Hunting spiders use their draglines to swing down to the ground from high places.

A bolas spider "fishing" for a moth. The bolas spider does not spin a silken web. Instead, it spins a line of silk with a drop of sticky silk at the end. The spider swings the line at its prey, trapping the moth on the sticky ball.

The labyrinth spider spins a tangled web to hide in, and an orb web to catch insects. The spider holds onto trap lines that tremble when an insect is caught in the orb web.

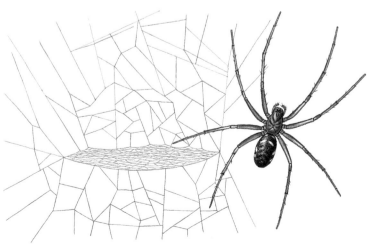

The platform spider spins a silk sheet below a net of criss-crossed threads. Flying insects hit the net and fall onto the sheet.

Spider courtship

Most spiders live alone. A male spider has to be very careful when he seeks a mate. The female spider may mistake him for prey, and eat him. Most male spiders perform courtship displays so that females will recognize them. Some dance, waving their legs and bodies. Some shake the female spider's web. Some even offer the female a gift – a captured fly.

Spider parents

Female spiders lay eggs. Most spiders enclose their eggs in a silken egg sac. Some mother spiders stay with the eggs, or even carry them around. A few kinds of mother spiders keep the young in their web for a time. Mother and young share the captured insects.

A crab spider on a flower. Some crab spiders can change slowly from white to yellow, to match the flowers on which they hide. When an insect lands on the flower, the spider strikes.

Blown to the ground. Spiderlings hatch from eggs inside the sac. They make holes in the side, and immediately begin to spin draglines. Caught by the wind, many travel to other areas, where food may be more plentiful.

A **jumping spider** leaps into the air to seize flying insects. The spider then floats down to the ground on its dragline.

How far can spiders jump? **Jumping spiders creep up and pounce on their prey. Despite its short legs, a jumping spider can jump more than 40 times the length of its own body!**

Why is a spider not trapped by its own web? **A web-spinning spider has a special hooked claw on each foot. When walking across the web, it grasps the silk lines with the hooks, so it never gets stuck.**

How does a spider know it has caught a meal? **Most web-spinning spiders have poor eyesight. They respond to the movement of the web when an insect becomes caught. Some attach a special trap line to the web. The spider hides in its nest near the web, holding on to the line. When it feels a tug (like an angler feeling a fish on the line), the spider darts out to capture its prey.**

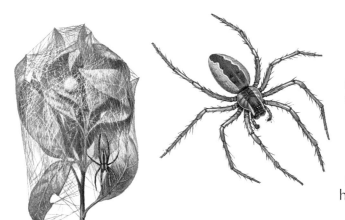

Ballooning off

Baby spiders sometimes travel long distances from home. They climb to the top of a fence post or bush, and tilt their spinnerets up into the air. The moving air pulls silk threads out of the spinnerets and off the spider flies, like a balloon at the end of a string. This unusual way of leaving home is called "ballooning."

A **female fisher spider** guards her egg sac. This spider spins a special nursery web in which to put her eggs. Fisher spiders can walk on water without sinking, and also make short dives underwater. They hunt water insects, small fish, and tadpoles.

Baby spiders are called spiderlings. The female wolf spider drags her eggs behind her in a sac, and when they hatch, the babies ride on their mother's back.

A kite spider from Africa has a large, two-spined head shield. Spiders may be various shapes – short and fat, long and thin, round, oblong, or flat.

ogre-faced stick spider

wolf spider

Nightmare faces. Are you glad that spiders are small creatures? These faces of spiders look scary, seen in close up. Spiders use pairs of graspers, called chelicerae, to seize their prey. Each chelicera ends in a hard, hollow claw. These claws are the fangs. When a spider stabs an insect with its chelicerae, poison flows through the fangs into the wound. The insect is either paralyzed or killed.

The king and the spider

People have always found spiders interesting. They are fascinated by the spider's skill at spinning webs, as well as by its skill as a hunter. A famous story tells how a Scottish king, Robert Bruce, was inspired by a spider.

Bruce was born in 1274, when England and Scotland were separate countries, and often at war. A legend tells how Bruce was hiding from his enemies in a wretched hut. He saw a spider swinging from the roof by one of its threads. It was trying to swing from one roof beam to another. It tried six times, and failed. Bruce realized he had fought six losing battles against the English. He watched to see if the spider would try again. It did, and on the seventh swing, the spider succeeded. Bruce took heart from the spider's success. He went off to fight again and won a famous victory.

Pets and nightmares

Some people like keeping large, hairy spiders as pets. Others would not willingly pick up the smallest house spider. They shriek and shudder. Yet most spiders are harmless, and usually keep well out of the way of people.

Tarantulas are the biggest spiders. Some tarantulas that live in South America can give a nasty bite. But the tarantulas that live in the United States are quiet creatures that live in burrows. A bite from one of these tarantulas is no worse than a bee sting. When annoyed, they rub their hind legs to fling into the air thousands of tiny body hairs. The hairs irritate the skin of an enemy.

Scorpions, Mites, Ticks

Scorpions, mites, and ticks are animals related to spiders.

Scorpions

Scorpions prefer warm climates. About 20 kinds live in the United States and Canada. A scorpion has eight legs, like a spider, but its body is a different shape. It has two tiny pincers near its head, and two large claws. At the tip of the scorpion's slender tail is a poisonous sting. When hunting, the scorpion seizes its prey in its claws, and then curls its tail over its head to sting the prey to death. Scorpions eat insects and spiders, and are most active at night. Mother scorpions give birth to live young, and the baby scorpions ride on their mother's back for several days.

A scorpion grabs prey with its powerful claws.

Mites

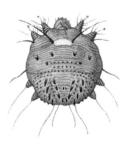

The itch mite has a baglike body.

Some mites are too small to be seen without a microscope. Many kinds of mites are parasites – harmful pests that suck the blood of animals or the juices of plants. Other mites eat feathers, cheese, and flour. Mites burrow into the skins of animals such as horses, cattle, and poultry, and humans too. However, many mites are useful. They live in the soil and help break down dead plant and animal matter.

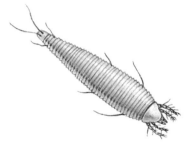

The pearleaf blister mite damages fruit trees.

Ticks

Ticks are bigger than mites. When a tick egg hatches, a flat larva with six legs crawls out. It waits on a grass stalk or shrub until an animal passes by. Then the tick clings onto the animal, pierces the animal's skin with its beak, and begins to feed on blood. The larva grows into an eight-legged nymph, and then into an adult tick, still hanging onto its host. Some ticks carry diseases.

A sheep tick becomes swollen with blood after it has eaten.

Facts and Records

The world of insects and spiders is full of amazing facts. Here are just a few.

Keen eyes. Some dragonflies have as many as 30,000 lenses in each eye.

Sweet tasters. Butterflies can taste the tiniest amounts of sugar in water. The amount of sugar detected by a monarch butterfly would have to be 2,000 times stronger before a person could taste it.

A tarantula. South American tarantulas are the world's largest spiders. With legs at full stretch, these spiders measure up to 10 inches (25 centimeters). Tarantulas have a longer life span than most other spiders. Some live more than 20 years.

Fast fliers. The fastest-flying insects are probably dragonflies. Some scientists estimate that these insects can fly as fast as 60 miles (97 kilometers) per hour.

Long-distance fliers. Butterflies and locusts can fly more than 100 miles (160 kilometers) without stopping to eat. They use food energy stored in their bodies. Tiny fruit flies can fly for more than five hours without needing to feed. A honey bee can fly for only 15 minutes before it needs to rest and refuel.

Changing skins. Insects and spiders shed their skins as they grow. A tarantula spider sheds its skin more than 20 times.

Dragonflies are speedy fliers.

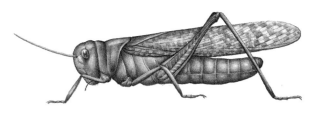

A locust. A swarm of locusts may contain many millions of insects like this one.

Biggest crowd. A swarm of locusts seen near the Red Sea was so enormous that it was believed to cover an area five times the size of New York City! Locust swarms have been seen flying far out at sea, more than 1,000 miles (1,600 kilometers) from land.

The Goliath beetle is one of the largest and heaviest insects. It is shown here life size. The Goliath beetle lives in Africa.

Mini-muscles. Large butterflies flutter their wings quite slowly – as few as 4 wingbeats a second. Some tiny midges beat their wings 1,000 times a second. These midges' wing muscles are probably the fastest-working muscles in the insect world!

The longest insects are probably walkingsticks. Some are over 12 inches (30 centimeters) long.

Robbers and slavers. Thief ants live by stealing food from other ants. Many ants also raid other ants' nests and carry off the young, which they bring up in their own nest as slaves.

One of the smallest insects is the fairy fly. It can barely be seen by the unaided eye. This picture shows a fairy fly greatly enlarged.

A queen termite may live as long as 50 years and is probably the longest-lived of all insects. When swollen with eggs, the queen termite grows to more than 4 inches (10 centimeters) long. She can lay at a rate of 10,000 to 30,000 eggs a day!

61

Glossary

abdomen The third and last section of the body of an insect.

antenna One of a pair of long feelers on the head of an insect.

arachnid A class of arthropod animals that includes spiders, scorpions, and mites.

arthropod An animal with jointed legs, such as an insect, crab, or spider.

beeswax Yellow substance made by honeybees, which they use to build honeycombs.

camouflage A disguise, such as a pattern or coloring, which makes an animal blend in with the background.

cell A small room; the wax structure in which bees store honey. A cell is also the tiny unit of living matter that makes up all animals and plants.

chitin Tough, horny material that makes up most of the outer covering or exoskeleton of insects.

colony A group of animals of the same kind living together, such as ants.

community A group of animals (or people) living together in the same area.

compound eye Eye made up of many tiny lenses or facets, each sending a different image to the brain.

crustacean An animal with a hard outer shell, including lobster, crab, or shrimp.

enzyme A substance found in living cells that causes a change in a biological process.

exoskeleton A skeleton that is outside the body, as in insects.

fertilization In reproduction, when male and female egg cells combine to form a new living thing.

fossil The remains of an animal from the distant past, preserved by becoming hard as rock.

fungi Plural of *fungus*. Plantlike living things that are not green, have no flowers or leaves, and absorb food from their surroundings.

halteres Rodlike balancing organs that help flies fly.

heredity The passing on of characteristics from parents to their offspring.

hibernation State of deep sleep and inactivity through winter.

insecticide Chemical used to kill insects.

instinct Behavior that is inherited, or comes naturally, rather than being learned.

larva The stage early in an insect's life when it looks like a worm.

maggot Larva of a fly.

mandibles Biting and crushing mouthparts used by insects for seizing and eating food.

mimic To copy or imitate something.

migration Leaving one place to settle in another. Some animals *migrate*.

nectar A sweet substance found in many flowers.

parasite A plant or animal that lives on another plant or animal, and takes its food from it.

pollen The yellow dust made in plants and found in a part of the flower. This dust is made up of male cells. It is carried by the wind, insects, or birds, and fertilizes the female parts of flowers so as to form seeds.

pollination Carrying pollen from one flower to another.

predator An animal that preys, or feeds on, other animals.

prehistoric Belonging to a time before the recording of history began.

pupa Stage in an insect's development between larva and adult.

resin A sticky substance that comes from trees and other plants.

saliva A clear liquid made in the mouth by certain glands. It helps with chewing, swallowing, and digesting food.

segment A section or part of a whole thing.

social insects Insects that live together in colonies, such as ants, bees, and termites.

species A group of living things with similar characteristics. Animals of the same species can breed with one another.

spinnerets A spider's silk-making organs.

spiracles Hollow tubes in the body through which insects breathe.

sterilize To make an animal or plant sterile, or unable to reproduce.

thorax The middle section of an insect's body.

ultraviolet Rays of light invisible to people, but not to some insects. Ultraviolet rays lie just beyond the violet end of the visible light spectrum.

Index A page number in **bold** type indicates a picture

Picture acknowledgments

Cover photo: Hermann Eisenbeiss, ABF.

4 Ron Larsen, Van Cleve Photography; 7 © David Scharf (top), Grant Hellman; 8 Hans Reinhard, Bruce Coleman; 9 Edward S. Ross; 12 A. J. Deane, Bruce Coleman; 14 Kjell B. Sandved, Bruce Coleman; 15 Grant Hellman (left), © Harry Rogers, Photo Researchers; 20, 21 Edward S. Ross; 23 (top) Shaw, APF; 23 (bottom) World Book photo by Don Stebbing; 24 (top) Eric Grave; 24 (bottom) Ross E. Hutchings; 25 (top) Thomas Eisner, (bottom) Bob Gossington, Bruce Coleman; 26 (top) Ross E. Hutchins, (bottom) Edward S. Ross; 28 Edward S. Ross; 29 (top) Jane Burton, Bruce Coleman, (middle) Bruce Coleman, (bottom) Edward S. Ross; 30 Ross E. Hutchins; 31 (top) Edward S. Ross, (bottom) John R. Conway; 32 Grace A. Thompson, N.A.S.; 33 Jane Burton; 34, © Anthony Bannister, N.H.P.A.; 36 Breck Kent, Animals Animals; 37 (top) Alexander B. Klots (right) Frank Roche, Animals Animals, (bottom) Edward S. Ross; 38 J. Shaw, Bruce Coleman; 39 Lacz Lemoine, N.H.P.A.; 40 Thomas Eisner; 41 (top) Alexander B. Klots, (bottom) James P. Rowan; 40 Edward S. Ross; 41 (top) Edward S. Ross, (bottom) Jan Taylor, Bruce Coleman; 44 (top) Edward S. Ross, (bottom) British Crown Copyright; 45 (top) Glen Sherwood, (bottom) Edward S. Ross; 46 Grant Hellman; 48 World Book (bottom, courtesy Field Museum of Natural History); 49 (top) Annan Photo, (left) Edward S. Ross, (right, top) © Stephen Dalton, Photo Researchers, (right, below) © Hans Rogers, Photo Researchers; 51 (top) Life Magazine © Time Inc.; Edward S. Ross; 52 Oxford Scientific Films; 53 Hans Pfletschinger from Peter Arnold; 58 John Visser, Bruce Coleman; 59 Kim Taylor, Bruce Coleman.

Illustrations

From WORLD BOOK by artists including Tom Dolan, John F. Eggert, Jack J. Kunz, Jasmes Teason, and Shirley Hooper; and by Jackie Harland.